W9-BNN-119

WORLD WAR II

NAVIES OF WORLD WAR II

Mike Taylor

Visit us at
www.abdopub.com

Published by Abdo Publishing Company, 4940 Viking Drive, Edina, MN 55435.
Copyright ©1998 by Abdo Consulting Group, Inc. International copyrights
reserved in all countries. No part of this book may be reproduced in any form
without written permission from the publisher.

Printed in the United States.

Interior Graphic Design: John Hamilton
Cover Design: MacLean & Tuminelly
Contributing Editors: John Hamilton; Morgan Hughes
Illustrations: John Hamilton, page 10
Cover photo: Digital Stock
Interior photos: Digital Stock, pages 1, 4, 5, 11, 13, 18, 19, 20, 23, 28, 31
            Corbis, pages 6, 14, 17, 18, 19, 21, 24, 26, 27
            U.S. Naval Historical Center, page 9

Sources: Boyne, Walter J. *Clash of Titans: World War II at Sea.* New York:
Simon & Schuster, 1994; Churchill, Winston S. *The Second World War.* 6 vols.
New York, 1948-1953; Stokesbury, James L. *A Short History of World War II.*
New York: William Morrow and Company, 1980; Wright, Gordon. *The Ordeal of
Total War, 1939-1945.* New York: Harper & Row, 1968.

Library of Congress Cataloging–in–Publication Data

Taylor, Mike, 1965-
    Navies of World War II / Mike Taylor
        p. cm. — (World War II)
    Includes index.
    Summary: Describes some of the ships used by the German, Japanese,
American, and British navies in World War II and the military strategies that led
to the defeat of the Axis powers.
    ISBN 1-56239-807-5
    1. World War, 1939-1945—Juvenile literature. [1. World War, 1939-1945—
Naval operations.] I. Title. II. Series: World War II (Edina, Minn.)
D743.7.T395   1998
940.53—dc21
                                            98-14184
                                                CIP
                                                AC

CONTENTS

Victorious American warships sail near Mount Fujiyama, Japan.

The USS *Pennsylvania* leads a battleship task force.

World War II began in 1939. The three members of the Axis powers, Germany, Italy, and Japan, scored tremendous victories at the beginning of the war against the Allied powers. After a devastating blow to American ships in Pearl Harbor on December 7, 1941, the United States joined forces with Great Britain. To ensure a victory, the Allied powers knew that they not only needed control over land and air, but also over the seas.

The British and U.S. navies fought the Axis powers with gigantic ships and aircraft carriers. Great battles were won and lost on oceans and seas across the globe. The U.S. and Great Britain's navies brought devastation to the Axis powers, and made Allied victories possible. Sailors fought on warships filled with cannons, and on submarines armed with torpedoes.

Both Axis and Allied powers were crippled by the tremendous battles fought on and under water. Many brave captains and soldiers lost their lives in naval warfare. In the end, ground troops eventually took over Germany and Japan, but it was the many battles fought by the navies of the Allied powers that made the final victory possible.

A sailor aboard the USS *Sandlance* sends a signal to another ship.

 5

THE FIRST BATTLES AT SEA

The *Graf Spee* burns after being scuttled by the Germans.

The era of World War II brought dramatic changes in naval warfare. The navies of the countries at war were much larger than ever before. The largest navies belonged to Great Britain and the United States of America.

Grand Admiral Karl Dönitz, supreme commander of the German navy, developed a strategy. Instead of trying to attack and defeat the British navy directly, Admiral Dönitz used Germany's warships to attack cargo ships moving food and weapons to Great Britain. In this way, Dönitz hoped to weaken Great Britain, forcing the country to surrender even though its navy was much larger.

German battleships prowled the Atlantic Ocean waiting to ambush unarmed British cargo ships. In 1939 the German ship *Graf Spee* (a *pocket battleship*, smaller than a regular battleship, but with powerful guns and thick armor) began a series of raids along the Atlantic coast of South America, as well as off the west coast of Africa and around the Cape of Good Hope. The *Graf Spee*, commanded by Captain Hans Langsdorff, sank nine cargo ships in two months and seemed unstoppable.

Captain Langsdorff was very skilled. Often, Langsdorff camouflaged his ship to look like a friendly vessel. The *Graf Spee* then snuck up on enemy cargo ships, often capturing their crew before they could destroy important documents. After the crew and supplies were transferred to the *Graf Spee* or its supply ship, the enemy cargo ship was then sunk.

Finally, on December 12, 1939, British ships caught up to the *Graf Spee*. Langsdorff was confident because his ship was larger and had bigger guns than any of the British ships in the area. The British ships, however, were much faster. The *Exeter*, the *Achilles,* and the *Ajax* easily caught the *Graf Spee*. The *Graf Spee* shot well and set the *Exeter* ablaze. Still, the *Exeter* stayed afloat to fire its torpedoes at the German battleship, which took more than 50 direct hits.

The *Ajax* hit the *Graf Spee* twice and put a large hole in the bow. Its fuel tanks were damaged and leaking badly. Captain Langsdorff himself was knocked unconscious by flying metal. Finally, several hours later, more British ships arrived to trap the *Graf Spee* in the harbor at Montevideo, Uruguay, where Captain Langsdorff sought fuel and repairs. Seeing no

 7

chance for escape, Langsdorff destroyed his own ship with bombs rather than surrender it to the British. Several days later, ashamed of losing his ship, Langsdorff killed himself. (He also did not want to face Hitler, who was known to be harsh with his military leaders when they were defeated.)

Germany's largest battleship was the *Bismarck*. The *Bismarck* was 823 feet (251 m) long (2 times longer than a football field), and 118 feet (36 m) wide. It had eight 15-inch (38 cm) cannons accurate to 25 miles (40.2 km). Its armor plating was 12 inches (30.5 cm) thick, easily able to withstand cannon fire and torpedoes. And even with all that weight, the *Bismarck* was one of the fastest ships on the seas.

In order to move into the Atlantic Ocean to attack British and American convoy ships, the *Bismarck* first had to pass through the treacherous Denmark Strait between Iceland and Greenland. British sailors spotted the *Bismarck* and the *Prinz Eugen,* a smaller German ship, on May 23, 1940. Hoping to destroy the great *Bismarck*, the British called in their own battleship, the *Hood*. The *Hood* had been the most powerful ship in the world, but was now much smaller than the new battleships like the *Bismarck.*

The *Bismarck* fired a salvo of shots. A single 800-pound (363 kg) shell hit the *Hood* in its ammunition storage. Hundreds of tons of ammunition exploded and broke the ship into two pieces. The ship went down in minutes, killing more than 1,400 sailors. Only three crewmembers from the *Hood* were saved.

Two days later, British planes spotted the *Bismarck* speeding toward the Atlantic Ocean. The British had a small fleet in the area, including the small aircraft carrier *Ark Royal*. The tiny aircraft of the *Ark Royal*, called Swordfish, which were loaded with torpedoes, could hardly expect to sink the mighty *Bismarck*. However, they managed to hit the *Bismarck's* rudder with a torpedo, which made navigating the battleship extremely difficult. The *Bismarck* was forced to steam into the wind, heading directly toward the British task force.

Finally, the British battleships arrived to finish off the crippled *Bismarck*. They first destroyed the

A view of the stern (rear) of the *Bismarck*.

In a dramatic sea chase, the British finally hunted down and sank the mighty *Bismarck*.

Bismarck's cannons and then moved in closer to fire shells through the thick armor. The *Bismarck* was a fiery wreck, and the captain had no choice but to sink his own ship, just as Captain Langsdorff had sunk the *Graf Spee*. Only 107 sailors from a crew of 2,000 survived.

SUBMARINE WARFARE

Germany's most effective ships were its submarines, called U-boats. (The name comes from the German word "Unterseeboote," which means *under sea boat*.) Indeed, under the command of Grand Admiral Karl Dönitz, Germany perfected submarine warfare during World War II. The U-boats were small and slow compared to other ships. Each had a crew of 40 to 50 men. They had diesel engines for surface cruising. On the surface they could travel at only 20 knots, compared to the *Bismarck,* which could travel at 30 knots and was twice as big.

The diesel engines could not work when the U-boat was submerged because the engines needed air in order to run. Instead, the submerged U-boat used battery-powered electric engines. The electric engines made the ship even slower.

A torpedoed Japanese destroyer photographed through the periscope of an American submarine.

 11

Even though its speed was very slow, a U-boat could travel 130 miles (209 km) under water before surfacing. This allowed it to creep very close to cargo ships without being seen. At close range, the U-boat's torpedoes were deadly accurate.

One of the most dramatic raids by a German U-boat occurred on October 13, 1939. Captain Gunther Prien and the crew of the U-47 U-boat steered into the British harbor at Scapa in northern England. Sure that they would not be seen, Prien and his crew were able to sneak through the dangerous maze of ships, buoys, and anchor chains to pick out and sink the best British ship in the harbor.

They chose the *Royal Oak*, a large battleship comparable to the *Bismarck*. From 9,000 yards (8,230 m), very close range indeed, U-47 fired three torpedoes at the *Royal Oak* from its bow tubes, then turned and fired a fourth from the stern tube. Disappointed because the *Royal Oak* was not sinking, Prien turned the U-boat around and attacked a second time.

Meanwhile, the captain of the *Royal Oak* could not believe that there was a German submarine in the harbor and thought the damage was caused by an engine explosion, or, at worst, a bomb from a German plane. They did nothing to defend against a second attack. This time Prien moved to only 4,800 yards (4,389 m) and fired three torpedoes, two of which hit point blank into the *Royal Oak*. The *Royal Oak* exploded and sank within fifteen minutes.

Gradually, British ships began to travel in large convoys of hundreds of vessels. With the cargo ships traveling close together, it was easier for the navy warships to defend against German submarine ambushes. Allied convoys used aircraft to spot U-boats from above. When submarines were found, bombs and depth charges were launched from the planes, but direct hits were rare. Gradually, however, the Allied forces began to reverse the early successes of the U-boat fleet.

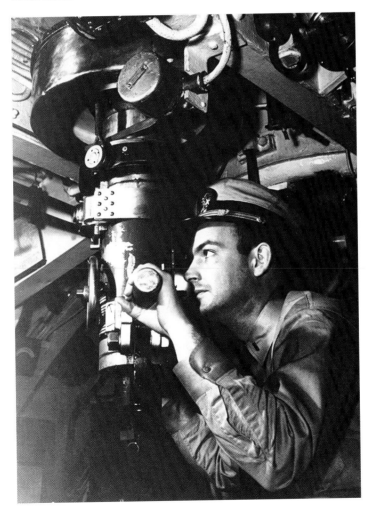

An officer peers through the periscope of an American submarine.

PEARL HARBOR

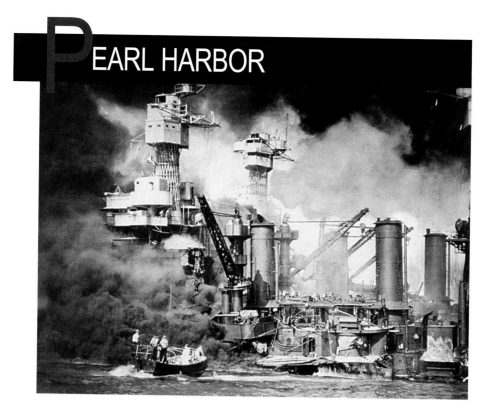

The battleships USS *West Virginia* and *Tennessee* sit low in the water and burn after the Japanese surprise attack on Pearl Harbor.

Just as Germany hoped to conquer the Atlantic Ocean with naval power, so did Germany's ally Japan hope to conquer the Pacific Ocean. Japan had already conquered large amounts of territory from China. Now Japan hoped to conquer the islands of the South Pacific, especially the Philippine Islands, owned by the United States. Over the years Japan had developed a very good navy, one of the best in the world, to accomplish its goals.

The heart of the Japanese navy was its 10 great aircraft carriers. These great ships, many of them dwarfing even the largest battleships, could carry as many as 70 planes. Elevators moved the planes from the flight deck to the service decks below, where they were fueled and repaired. This protected the planes and kept the flight deck clear so that the deadly "Zero"

fighter planes could land safely. When the war began the Japanese had the best aircraft carriers in the world.

In addition to its aircraft carriers, the Japanese navy had 10 large battleships and several hundred smaller warships. While Japan's navy was substantially smaller than the navies of Great Britain and the United States, Japan did not need so large a fleet. Japan's ships were all concentrated in the Pacific Ocean, while the larger navies were spread all over the world.

Japan regarded the United States as the only obstacle to its plans for the South Pacific islands. Indeed, the United States had blocked shipments of oil to Japan, hoping to slow the expansion of the Japanese empire and deprive its navy of fuel. Therefore, Japan's leaders concluded that Japan must attack and defeat the United States before conquering the islands.

Most important among Japan's leaders was the grand admiral of the navy, Isoruku Yamamoto. It was Yamamoto who planned the infamous Japanese surprise attack on Pearl Harbor on December 7, 1941. Yamamoto planned to send a fleet of six aircraft carriers and six cruisers toward Pearl Harbor.

The carriers would be accompanied by numerous battleships and submarines, 25 attack vessels in all. Each Japanese submarine carried on its back a midget submarine piloted by a single crewman. The miniature submarines could creep undetected with torpedoes even into the shallow water of Pearl Harbor.

At 6:00 a.m. the Japanese planes began to leave the aircraft carriers. Among the numerous types of planes, the most important were the "Val" divebombers and "Zero" fighter planes. The Zero was the best fighter plane in the war, and the Vals were as effective as Germany's famous Stuka dive bomber.

The U.S. Navy was taken utterly by surprise. The excellent U.S. battleship fleet, seven of its best ships, were lined up neatly in port. Hundreds of planes were lined up along runways at several small airfields. All of these made very easy targets.

The Japanese fighters and bombers destroyed most of the American planes before they could leave the ground. This made it impossible to defend the American battleship fleet in the harbor.

The *West Virginia* was hit by several bombs and torpedoes in the first minutes of the attack. While the ship was sinking, its crew adjusted the counterweight ballast to help it settle evenly. The *West Virginia* settled evenly in the shallow water. Most of its crew survived and its guns kept blazing from the deck, still 20 feet (6 m) above water!

The heroism could not prevent the Japanese victory, however. Japanese dive bombers were deadly accurate. The *Arizona* was hit by a single bomb that sailed directly into one of its great gun turrets. The *Arizona's* own ammunition exploded so violently that the ship was broken into pieces and sunk instantly. Nearly all of her crew, more than 1,000 strong, were trapped inside and drowned in the burning oil slick.

Only four hours after the attack began, the shocked American survivors measured the damage. Five other U.S. battleships, the *Oklahoma*, the *California*, the

Tennessee, the *Maryland*, and the *Nevada*, were badly damaged. Three destroyers were damaged beyond repair. Three cruisers had been damaged as well. Almost 300 U.S. airplanes had been destroyed on the ground. The attack killed 2,403 men, 1,178 of them from the *Arizona*. It was only luck that had kept America's own aircraft carriers away from the harbor and safely out to sea.

Less than one week after the surprise attack on Pearl Harbor, U.S. President Franklin Roosevelt declared war on Japan immediately and on Germany a few days later. But with its best fighting ships damaged in Pearl Harbor, it would be months before the U.S. could threaten Japan. In the meanwhile, the Japanese fleet began to overrun the islands of the South Pacific, including the Philippine Islands.

The USS *Arizona* explodes in flames, killing 1,178 American sailors.

1939 September 1: Battle of Poland. German *Blitzkrieg* overwhelms Poland with high-speed tanks and aircraft. The Battle of Poland was the beginning of World War II.

1939 December: German Battleship *Graf Spee* sunk after a battle with British ships off South America.

1940 May: Massive battleships *Hood* (British) and *Bismarck* (German) sunk.

1941-1942: German "U-boats" dominate the Atlantic Ocean.

1941 December 7: Japanese surprise attack on Pearl Harbor, Hawaii. Japanese aircraft carriers stage successful surprise attack and destroy much of the American fleet at Pearl Harbor in Hawaii. Because

the Japanese used strict radio silence, it was impossible for the Americans to intercept messages and predict the attack.

1942 May: U.S. Victory over Japan in the Battle of the Coral Sea.

18

1942 June: U.S. victory over Japan in the Battle of Midway Island. One of the greatest battles among aircraft carriers. Japanese aircraft carriers attacked, but the Americans were prepared and won the battle decisively. The

Americans sank four Japanese aircraft carriers. The Japanese sank one American carrier, the *Yorktown*.

1943: Allied Powers improve their anti-submarine weapons in the Atlantic.

1944 June 6: "D-Day," the Allied invasion of France. Allied forces use hundreds of small landing craft to attack the beaches of northern France. The Allies land so many soldiers in this way that they eventually liberate Paris and push the Germans out of France.

1945 May 8: V-E Day. Victory in Europe! The Germans surrender to the Allies.

1945 August 14: Japan surrenders to the Allies after witnessing the terrible destruction in the cities of Hiroshima and Nagasaki. The surrender documents are signed by Japanese representatives aboard the USS *Missouri*.

CARRIER WARFARE

A U.S. Army B-25 takes off from the deck of a U.S. Navy aircraft carrier on its way to a bombing run over Tokyo, Japan.

The Japanese success at Pearl Harbor proved the tremendous value of a good aircraft carrier fleet. Luckily, the American aircraft carriers did not suffer any damage at all. The most important battles in the Pacific during the remainder of the war were between aircraft carriers. The planes did most of the fighting, while the huge ships rarely came within sight of each other.

Another conclusion of the Pearl Harbor disaster was that the United States began to build new ships at so fast a pace as to amaze the world. The new ships were of the highest quality and fitted with the best radar equipment and weapons.

Furthermore, the United States worked diligently to intercept and decode Japanese radio signals. During the spring of 1942, specialists in radio espionage concluded that Japan would soon attempt to conquer

Australia and that they would use the Coral Sea, northeast of Australia, as a stepping stone. Admiral Chester Nimitz, commander of the U.S. fleet in the Pacific, prepared to ambush the Japanese fleet in the Coral Sea.

The U.S. attack force included two aircraft carriers, the *Lexington* and the *Yorktown*, along with the destroyer *Minneapolis* and numerous smaller ships. The aircraft were mostly "Dauntless" dive bombers and "Devastator" torpedo bombers.

On May 5, 1942 a group of Japan's prized aircraft carriers, *Shokaku* and *Zuikaku*, under the command of Rear Admiral Takeo Takagi entered the Coral Sea. The *Yorktown* and *Lexington* were waiting. Dauntless dive bombers from the *Lexington* sank the Japanese carrier *Shoho* quickly. Meanwhile, Japanese bombers

A Japanese warship is under heavy fire from U.S. aircraft.

 21

searched frantically for the American carriers. In the dark, Japanese planes mistakenly tried to land on the American carrier *Yorktown* because they mistook it for their own home ship!

The next day, the dive bombers nearly sank the Japanese carrier *Shokaku*. The crippled *Shokaku* did not sink, but finally limped away in flames, leaving its planes to crash into the sea.

Meanwhile, the *Yorktown* and the *Lexington* were themselves under heavy attack from Japanese bombers. The *Lexington* was engulfed in flames and had to be abandoned when its stores of aviation fuel exploded. Finally, an American destroyer sank the burning *Lexington* with torpedoes so that the Japanese could not salvage it for their own use.

The battle of the Coral Sea was a large victory for the United States, which had prevented the Japanese from conquering the Coral Sea, but had lost one of its aircraft carriers, the *Lexington*. A larger victory was needed, however, to turn the tide of the war against Japan.

That opportunity arose only a month later when the Japanese attacked Midway Island, an American island northwest of Hawaii. Japanese Admiral Yamamoto believed that capturing the island would make the entire Pacific Ocean safer for the Japanese navy.

Just as in the Coral Sea, however, American experts had decoded Japanese radio signals and predicted the Japanese attack.

On June 4, when the attack began, the United States had an overwhelming fleet of aircraft carriers prepared to defend Midway Island. Dive bombers from the *Enterprise* attacked the Japanese carriers *Kaga*, *Akagi*, and *Soryu*. All three were set on fire, their crews trapped and burned by gasoline fires hot enough to turn the steel red. Torpedoes from a U.S. submarine finally broke up the *Soryu* and sank it.

Sailors scramble to put out a raging fire aboard the aircraft carrier USS *Bunker Hill*.

By the end of the next day, the Battle of Midway had turned into a huge victory for the United States. The United States lost one aircraft carrier, the *Yorktown*, and one destroyer, along with nearly 150 planes. The Japanese lost four aircraft carriers along with most of their planes and countless other ships.

Just as important was the fact that the United States was beginning to produce new ships and planes much more quickly than they were being destroyed. After the Battle of Midway, the carrier war in the Pacific Ocean turned quickly in favor of the United States.

VICTORY IN THE ATLANTIC

The U.S. battleship *Missouri* ("Mighty Mo") fires a broadside with its 16-inch guns.

Just as the growing United States Navy helped to turn the tide against Japan in the Pacific Ocean during 1942, so did it help to turn the tide against Germany in the Atlantic Ocean the next year.

Many factors contributed to the victory of the Allies in the Atlantic. Among the most important factors was that the British had broken the German naval code just as the Americans had broken the Japanese code. German submarine captains used a tool called the Enigma Machine to transfer normal German language into code before a radio message was sent. They were confident that the British could never break the Enigma Machine's code. However, the British captured an Enigma Machine. Expert mathematicians

24

in England studied the complicated tool until they understood the code it produced, and the radio messages among German submarines. This allowed them to predict submarine attacks and prepare defenses for the ship convoys.

The convoys themselves were stronger as well. The earliest convoys had very few planes. Many of these planes were launched from catapults instead of runways. Because the ships had no runways, the planes had to leave after a very short time to land in Greenland far to the north.

The new aircraft carriers, mostly from the United States, had full runways and storage for airplanes below deck. Of course, it was not easy to land a plane even on these larger carriers. The waves caused the runway to rise and fall as much as 50 feet (15m) during takeoffs and landings! The new ships were far superior, though, carrying many more planes and covering each convoy with hundreds of aircraft.

Great improvements were made in the use of radar in 1943. A radar unit measures the distance of an object by measuring the amount of time needed for a sound wave to reach the object and return to the unit. By 1943 the Allied powers had radar units in every convoy, with a range that reached out to 12 miles (19 km). These were far superior to any German or Japanese units.

Indeed, most German submarines did not have any radar at all. That fact, combined with the new aircraft carriers, allowed the Allied powers to go on the

 25

Nazi sailors cringe around the conning tower of a German U-boat under attack by American planes. A few minutes later, the U-boat took a direct hit and was sunk.

offensive and begin hunting the submarines. U-boats would wait in ambush as always. Now, however, Allied radar would locate the submarines well in advance. Planes could be sent out in front to bomb the U-boats before they ever saw the Allied ships.

Depth charges, bombs set to explode at a certain depth under water, were used against U-boats. Earlier, the depth charges could only be rolled overboard, and were very inaccurate. Now, they could be dropped by the dozens from airplanes with greater accuracy.

With depth charges exploding all around, a U-boat captain had to decide whether to surface and surrender, or be exploded under water. Fearing the anger of the German leader Adolf Hitler, the captains often chose to fight to the death rather than surrender.

In all of 1942, the Allies managed to sink only one German submarine. In 1943, they sank nearly 200! All of these factors helped the Allied powers turn the struggle for control of the Atlantic Ocean to their favor by the end of 1943.

Sailors on the deck of the U.S. Coast Guard cutter *Spencer* watch the explosion of a depth charge, which blasted a Nazi U-boat's hope of breaking into the center of a large convoy.

CONCLUSION

The combined navies of Great Britain and the United States were very important in the defeat of Germany and Japan. Just as it was important to control the skies, it was also important to control the seas. Their control of the skies and the seas made possible the huge Allied invasion of France on "D-Day," June 6, 1944. Likewise, control of the air and seas made possible the U.S. victories in the South Pacific between 1942 and 1945, including the recapture of the Philippine Islands. While the Allied ground troops eventually occupied Germany and Japan, the Allied navies helped to make the victory possible.

Sailors salute a fallen comrade at a U.S. cemetery.

INTERNET SITES

A-Bomb WWW Museum
http://www.csi.ad.jp/ABOMB/index.html
   This site provides readers with accurate information concerning the impact of the first atomic bomb on Hiroshima, Japan.

Black Pilots Shatter Myths
http://www.af.mil/news/features/features95/f_950216-112_95feb16.html
   This site tells of the exploits of the 332nd Fighter Group, the first all-black flying unit known as the Tuskegee Airmen.

United States Holocaust Museum
http://www.ushmm.org/
   The official Web site of the U.S. Holocaust Memorial Museum in Washington, D.C.

What Did You Do In The War, Grandma?
http://www.stg.brown.edu/projects/WWII_Women/tocCS.html
   An oral history of Rhode Island women during World War II. In this project, 17 students interviewed 36 Rhode Island women who recalled their lives in the years before, during, and after the Second World War.

World War II Commemoration
http://gi.grolier.com/wwii/wwii_mainpage.html
   To commemorate the 50th anniversary of the end of the war, Grolier Online assembled a terrific collection of World War II historical materials on the Web. Articles taken from *Encyclopedia Americana* tell the story of World War II, including biographies. Also included are combat films, photographs, a World War II history test, and links to many other sites.

These sites are subject to change. Go to your favorite search engine and type in "World War II" for more sites.

Pass It On
   World War II buffs: educate readers around the country by passing on information you've learned about World War II. Share your little-known facts and interesting stories. We want to hear from you! To get posted on the ABDO & Daughters website, E-mail us at "History@abdopub.com"

Visit the ABDO & Daughters website at www.abdopub.com

GLOSSARY

Aircraft Carrier: Aircraft carriers were the largest ships by far in any fleet in World War II. They were equipped with runways on which fighter planes and small bombers could land and take off. This allowed for air battles far out into the ocean, like the Battle of the Coral Sea and the Battle of Midway in May and June of 1942.

Allies: The Allies were the many nations that were allied, or joined, in the fight against Germany, Italy, and Japan in World War II. The most powerful nations among the Allies included the United States, Great Britain, and the Soviet Union.

Axis powers: The Axis powers were the World War II alliance of Germany, Italy, and Japan.

Blitzkrieg: German word meaning "lightning warfare." Describes a new German military strategy in World War II. *Blitzkrieg* called for very large invasions to overwhelm the enemy quickly and avoid long, drawn out battles.

D-Day, June 6, 1944: Code name for the beginning of the great Allied attack on German forces in France.

Hiroshima: Name of the Japanese city where the United States dropped the first atomic bomb, on August 6, 1945. The city was destroyed.

Landing Craft: These were small boats used to transport troops from the larger ships up to the beaches during an attack. The landing craft was a small and simple weapon, but very important to the success of the great D-Day invasion on June 6, 1944, which led to the defeat of Germany.

U-boat: The name for Germany's deadly submarines in World War II. German U-boats were very effective during the Battle of the Atlantic between 1940 and 1942. However, by 1942 the Allies found ways to avoid the U-boats, and the Germans lost the Battle of the Atlantic.

V-E Day, May 8, 1945: After German leader Adolf Hitler committed suicide, the German generals surrendered on May 7. The United States proclaimed May 8 to be "V-E Day," which stood for "Victory in Europe."

A U.S. aircraft carrier is under attack by Japanese dive bombers at the Battle of Santa Cruz.

 31

NDEX

A
Achilles 7
Africa 7
aircraft carrier 5, 9, 14, 15, 17, 20-23, 25
Ajax 7
Akagi 23
Allied powers 4, 5, 13, 24-26, 28
Arizona, USS 16, 17
Ark Royal 9
Atlantic Ocean 6, 8, 9, 24, 26
Australia 21
Axis powers 4

B
battleship 6-9, 12, 14-16
Bismarck 8-12

C
California, USS 16
Cape of Good Hope 7
China 14
convoy 8, 13, 25
Coral Sea, Battle of 21, 22

D
D-Day 28
Dauntless dive bomber 21
Denmark Strait 8
depth charge 13, 26
destroyer 17, 21-23
Devastator torpedo bomber 21
Dönitz, Grand Admiral Karl 6, 11

E
Enigma Machine 24
Enterprise, USS 23
Exeter 7

G
Germany 4-6, 8, 11, 14, 16, 17, 24, 28
Graf Spee 6, 7, 10
Great Britain 4-6, 12, 15, 25, 28
Greenland 8, 25

H
Hitler, Adolf 8, 26
Hood 8

I
Iceland 8
Italy 4

J
Japan 4, 5, 14-17, 20-25, 28

K
Kaga 23

L
Langsdorff, Captain Hans 7, 8, 10
Lexington, USS 21, 22

M
Maryland, USS 17
Midway, Battle of 22, 23
Minneapolis, USS 21
Montevideo, Uruguay 7

N
Nevada, USS 17
Nimitz, Admiral Chester 21

O
Oklahoma, USS 16

P
Pacific Ocean 14, 14, 15, 17, 20, 21-24, 28
Pearl Harbor, Hawaii 4, 15, 17, 20
Philippine Islands 14, 17, 28
Prien, Captain Gunther 12
Prinz Eugen 8

R
radar 20, 25, 26
Roosevelt, President Franklin 17
Royal Oak 12

S
Shoho 21
Shokaku 21, 22
Soryu 23
South America 7
submarine 5, 11-13, 15, 23-26

T
Takagi, Rear Admiral Takeo 21
Tennessee, USS 17

U
U-boat 11, 12, 13, 26
United States 4, 6, 14, 15, 20, 22-25, 28

V
Val dive bomber 16

W
West Virginia, USS 16

Y
Yamamoto, Grand Admiral Isoruku 15, 22
Yorktown, USS 21-23

Z
Zero dive bomber 14, 16
Zuikaku 21